There is a delicate difference
to be found in all the beautiful ones
and we are beautiful ones--
Delicately different;
hand-picked by Love
For such a time as this

Flowering & Decaying

EMMANUELLA RAPHAELLE

Flowering & Decaying
Copyright © 2021 by Emmanuella Raphaelle
All rights reserved. Printed in the United States of America.
No part of this book may be used or reproduced in any manner
whatsoever without the written consent of the publisher, except
in the case of brief quotations used in reviews or scholarly
articles.

Published by Journal Journey LLC
ISBN: 978-0-9981741-3-6

Journal Journey books are available at discounted rates for bulk
purchases intended for educational, business, or promotional use.

For more information, please contact Emmanuella Raphaelle at:
erm@ermsJournal.com

For Michaelle, To Gabrielle

CONTENTS

INTERNAL INTERVALS
13

INSTINCT & IDENTITY
33

WORTHY WOMAN
55

POETIC POETRY
83

EPILOGUE
100

An ENTRY

She Left Us This Morning…

I went to see her last night.

There was a feeling surrounding me as I moved around in the comfort of a bright sun and the calm solace in my home. The feeling talked to me through different hours of the day, nudging me to dress my body and make haste to a place that had become routine in the last few weeks. I listened.

I went to see her last night.

I don't know that I will be the last loved one in her presence. What bothers me is I am not sure she sees me—for her eyes are fixated above and beyond…But seeing her this way will never leave me—of this, I am sure. I resolved as I walked out of her room, down the long monochromatic hall, out of the facility called Tranquility, I would see her no more.

No more is upon us. Joy came for her at seven this Sunday morning. Her body set her free. She had suffered long enough. Gallbladder cancer—that is how it started. A tumor in the brain is how it ended. I would know her no more in the way we had occupied sisterhood. She would no longer live, move and have her being with us on Earth.

It is afternoon. The close ones have gathered. The thread of love is sewing us closer in our garment of grief. Unto each other's bosom, there is much embracing and weeping.

Have you ever heard a wise woman pray while she cries? The words from her severed heart are pouring forth from her lips. Inconsolable, she beseeches and praises. It is truly gut-wrenching to hear the cries rise from the belly of the beloved.

Separation is hard. What an understatement. Because this sunder is unwanted and forever. But in all of our reasoning and entreating, we should not ask God why because, in essence, this question is without meaning. We are not exempt from the conditions of living.

An INTRODUCTION

This is not a book about grief. On the contrary, this is a book about living.

I've wrestled with opening words to introduce a complicated, vibrant life once been, who passed away one Fall, who some say continues in the ether in some form of way or other.

She was a mother, a friend, a high school counselor. She was a therapist, an entrepreneur. The oldest sister, she was a mentor. She believed big for me. She taught me how to wear heels.

I've wrestled with offering better-fitting words to debut the other, still breathing in her womanhood, living in our sisterhood. A complex feminine being inquiring, untelling, and unlearning her stories for substance to her believing and meaning.

She is a mother, a teacher, a friend. She is a defy-er and a supporter. She is a sister. She taught me resilience. She continues to teach me how to live big.

We were three sisters who grew up in Brooklyn, New York, and sojourned to Atlanta, GA, to grow up in ways unimaginable. Though different in our self-actualizations, one common theme threaded us—a heart for women.

With words whispered and spoken among us, prayed aloud, or murmured quietly, I give you access into *our*. This book is an offering to convince you to live.

Amidst *our,* wisdom and clarity, raw truth and honesty, interlined our vulnerability. Big sister always had something to say. Middle sister always had a question. And I, the youngest sister, have the words...I have the poetry.

I told her I would write for her. Today I make good on that word. Once this work is published, it will be a gift, a surprise homage to the one reading.

To every sister, who came, and who remains. Do not miss your life. And hold the hand of another sister while you can.

INTERNAL INTERVALS

Leap

Leap for joy because…
Why not?
You ought to
Leap into the new day with all the liveliness one can summon
Up and around like a young child
happy for rain, sunshine, mud, snow
Leap into the arms of love or a pile of leaves, a soft bed
Leap into every opportunity in its lifetime
Leap into action—you got things to do and much to achieve
Leap into life, leap into gratitude,
Leap into laughter, bliss, and beauty
Leap into the breath of your body—just breathe
Leap into your lessons
your experiences
your fears
your pleasures
Leap into your happy place
Leap into your life

We are all deserving of a human love
that blends our complicated into the simplest form
of soul-to-soul love
It won't be easy like Sunday morning every day
But it will be pleasing on most evenings after dawning
After we've replenished our soul with
a good fixing of mourning...
the loss of all things bland and bitter--
Then we can be sweet
and complicated, together
On the odd days and
the even

*What would happen if every human being on Earth
lived like a human being leaving Earth?*

The beauty of our brevity
is losing its luster,
giving way to a shadow of fear within me
But it is life's intensity
I want engulfing
the thoughts and spaces of me
Life's heavenly mercy I want
guiding and keeping me, us

Because the nothingness of death
un-nerves me
I want above all
for this to remain
stagnant behind me
so that I may
move on and along

So that I may
move on and along
move on with my one irresistible life
along all the perfect plans life has for me

If every human being lived like a human leaving
Perhaps we would be moved by the
beauty of our briefness
Perhaps we would move and have our being
kindly, eloquently, sincerely
Perhaps…

Because the nothingness of death un-nerves me...
If we could live Full in the meantime

Life has a way of "humiliating" us
Brings us low to our knees
Acquainting us with the lowest part of ourselves
where our deepest fears, anxieties
disappointed anticipations sit and lurk
Deep in the soft of us where
our unwants accumulate to gather
and burgeon
And in those humiliating moments
when the heart is captive,
the humble us can convene with compassion
and realize,
it is good to be beside ourselves
If only for a moment,
to keep us sober and vigilant
We will never arrive
We should never be too proud for too long
because for as long as we breathe
We will be going…to arrive

Pace yourself; Honor your journey

If only bitterness could be barren
if only we could relinquish regret
and relent the unloving way,
Cease to hoard our hearts
but rather engage in the generosity
of affection and kindness
Really partake in the fragility and
vulnerability of our soul...
To join, to amend, to commune
If all that, we could
so much more would be revealed
and availed to us
Our together is the way

Love may ask us to suffer long
through repentance and grace
through compassion and understanding
through peace and mercy
But not through the breaking of us
Not through the slow deterioration of us
No, that is not what love will beseech of us

Love will ask us to dwell in the vulgar of vulnerability
to be near a naked heart and not negate the renewable
Love will ask that we empty the offense
and yet rest in the embrace of our beloved
Yes, love will do that
Love will ask us to wear our Beloved's shoes,
Especially because they won't fit,
but are fit to give us in-sight

Love won't ask us to overlook, but rather
compel us to overcome
Love requires us to be honest and earnest
To be the salve in the struggle
And poignant in the peak
Giving gratitude in all seasons
It asks much of us,
Because much is required to enjoy
and endure it all
Love may ask us to suffer long—but only through love

Now then, who among us can stand to love?

From Metal Wings

And though we journey together,
each sojourn is different in destiny
We journey together to discover individualities
yet to be shown or seen
What a lovely place to be
in the space of impending discovery
I pray we all remember to allow the new things,
the different things to touch and amaze us
I wish we all remember to look at the world around us
from the eyes of absolute ignorance and awe
to be well in wonder
to be uncomfortable not knowing
yet comfortable in that
to not dumb down or turn our nose up to
the prospects around a corner
Because to not grasp the hand of hope
and share a heartbeat with it…
To not accept the invitation
to live in the uncertainty—
faithfully, wholeheartedly
is the true tragedy

remember to remember

how to be alone
like
the unborn fetus in the womb
quiet, fearless
trusting dark
guiding life

how to be together
like
yin and yang
male and female
rising, falling
thirsting, burning
belonging

we've forgotten

how to look to the stars
and believe
as it is in Heaven
so it is on Earth
this much love you can have
and more
promise

we ought to remember

how to recover
to see beyond the face

Emmanuella Raphaelle

hear beyond the voice
bypass the flesh
to the crux of the matter
in the heart
bear the cross

Intrigued
that love lives
still
within, beyond,
streams, hills, and clouds
along miles and acres and forests and lakes
through thresholds and buildings along walls and
tall open windows
through and around despite of
even though—
Persons exist
interrupt, interfere in the flow,
in the beam, in the light, in the atmosphere
the hemisphere
Love, it still carries us,
still circulates our breathing

Intrigued
that love lives
still
within, without
endures beyond the mistakes of the body,
the sins of the skin
the transgressions of thoughts
the doubts of stagnant limbs
through the skeptical heartbeat
and indecisive hands

Emmanuella Raphaelle

Love endures
beyond
the fear of the unknown
past the inequities of our illicit desires
and lucid dreams
Love still lives
to endure
not even caring about the limitations
of our small brains
our finite feelings

Love dares to
embolden and hold us
to an accountability
It scoffs at our smallness of being
it calls us out and up
towards the edge of uncharted colonies
and turbulent territories
It challenges us to
change towards chance
And to believe the truth of the message of
love endures
beyond us humans

muddy water

this morning's cup of coffee
tastes like a warm tide of indulgence
warming my chest
artificially sweetening life's current events
caramelizing all my not-so-good into
tolerable moments
bolder by the sip
life after a cup of coffee
and the world is not so muddy after all

my wish
for a world made of flesh
and other soft things
not of glass
nor stone
not of bullets--rubber or steel
not of clay or other can-be-broken things
disintegrating into the ether
but more like tenderness
penetrating time and space
touch and tenderness
that transcends the colors of a face
or hand
but meets at heart
where red bleeds and blends
a world of people-ness
you know, made of humanness...

If only we knew how holy we are;
that angels in Heaven rejoice over us
We would longer kiss those angels while they are still among us

All day God has been mourning
I wonder what grieves him more
that "thou shall not kill" has become a slogan for the restless
or that we are standing over the precious
with no understanding for life at all

My God has been teary-eyed all day
trapped in moments of sun clouded by our sin
for we have forgotten how to love our-
selves into loving each other
We've beguiled ourselves into thinking we are man-made
forsaking in His image
suffocating His breath of life ventilating our mass of flesh
that we are the mass coming together to fall apart

Each time and every time
my brother's keeper snatches God's breath from me
he bleeds from you
Later there will be dead flowers for all the
slain angels hovering between...
how many more...

Mother Earth is overcrowded with the spirits of men
turning to ash while we walk over them
dampening them with our tears

There was no sunshine today
but I have mourned enough for me
tomorrow, I will, breath for you

Supplicate

Sister
say a prayer for them
the ones who don't know hope
the ones living without
rest and comfortability
for the ones struggling through
for they know not
hope can come

the storms come to lift away
the loose things, the dead things
the debris in the details
loosening from us the implements
expired and weighty

let the storm pass

The Day

The day is diligent to remind us,
we are perfect for any moment,
diligent to be just as it is:
pure, un-feeling, nonjudgmental

The day is always free of expectations
and absolutions but always abundant
in mercy and calmness;

Always brimming with beauty and serendipity
offering a hand of serenity
a choice to flow in and out;
effortlessly in the details of the moment

The day is diligent, profound in its
neutrality
It simply asks us to partake
and impart only wholly and fully
in every moment
Because the day knows in all of these…
This too shall pass

INSTINCT & IDENTITY

Offer

Be open Darling,
Offer yourself as a living sacrifice, because you are
In all things, offer your best self—others need it
Offer kindness in truth
Offer integrity—we're running out
Offer a donation—the world needs it
Offer forgiveness—you need it
When you can, offer a hug, offer communion,
offer your heart—you can do that
Offer a helping hand or a purposeful prayer
Offer a word of wisdom and praise
Offer strength or good judgment
Offer clarity, offer character, offer curiosity
Offer yourself the wild chance to do and want all your heart desires
And as you offer yourself to the others
Remember, offer yourself too, a full dose of you

Words I give to myself amid each moment

I am the product of a foreign love
stifled yet strong
innocent
battered and bruised
resurrected
from the womb

I am the seed of a different love...
of a resilient rebellion
of broken language, bare feet, and aristocrat
born free to birth dreams
they didn't see

I am the child of immigrant love
the produce of a praying love

I am last daughter of once love

I won't compromise
and I don't apologize,
I want everything
good and perfect
for my soul

Emmanuella Raphaelle

The moon, full
I plucked it down from the sky
stared at the matchless marvel of it all
Held it in my clutch for a short moment
then let it go
for it would be selfish of me
to keep it all to my small self
But I am so big from the inside

He
makes
me
lie
down
in
soft
green
pastures,
because
the
wilderness
of
the
world,
would
swallow
me
whole...

Emmanuella Raphaelle

Love,
you have
given me
beautiful eyes
to behold within
Mask off, armor undone
to let pure Love pour in, through
skin, bones, and marrow, heart, and flesh
to let One Love, grow and forgive me
bound to my end, I love with everything

maybe
it was time to wake up...
the sun didn't malinger

no more should I

Emmanuella Raphaelle

And I rise from the shadows of a fallen tree
whose noble leaves did guide me along a trodden path
I rise with stems and roots of bitter hope in a short winter
sprung from a long fall where my letters and words did bear
witness to a when I become strong enough to go on my own
I rise with the sun and go with the wind, pen in hand to write
herstory co-authored by an angel in a cloud hosting me
I rise with a native love for a life almost taken abruptly
from them who claimed to love me cause
if I don't, no one will rise for me

But I am convinced
When I live in gratefulness,
the universe gives me more to be grateful for
I believe more and more
Gratitude attracts abundance of life and grace
To handle all the more God has in store
to give
me

Therefore,
I say Thank You
Because it is my practice
It is my spirituality

Emmanuella Raphaelle

I fell in love this morning
it was so sudden
but I knew this love would endure for longer than a moment
maybe it was the way the dawning fell upon her brown skin
or the way the autumn's dying breath slipped through fine hairs
goosebumps telling on flesh
a nervous system hiding butterflies on the inside

I fell in love this morning
so deep in love
with a woman
soulful, humble in her being
tired but willing to push through living
and it's not complicated but beautiful
for I know,
no other will ever love me like this again

Preview

After soft rain washed away tears,
I turned wiser
I know better to do better,
I am the change
No longer protected in a cocoon,
mature butterfly
Time tells no lies and actions
I do believe
Breakthrough…
and everything is a brilliant yellow
Broken pieces of vinyl,
but
new lyrics
new song

Do Good Anyway

Life has taught me
there will be
men afraid to love me
and that is well
There will be
women who are unkind to me
and that is well
I will love me
I will be kind to me
and I will love them kindly
that is my duty
to extend that which is denied me
I understand,
in the world, there will be
secondary characters and spectators
who misjudge me,
misappropriate me,
nail labels to me
and that is fine
I will not judge them inappropriately
Nor accept or crucify with labels their identity
Instead to do good anyway and not grow weary
That is the way I will persist
That is my duty
To extend mercy
To extend empathy
To extend charity
to the ones who make it harder
to endure my own humanity

Because in this life I have learned
it is possible to live up to my Calling
and not their falling

I do not live in my past
I live in God's presence

And in His presence
I live in the sunrise of my brown eyes…
and all the small and meaningful
miraculous gifts He imparts
to my heart daily
I take them in completely
releasing an unapologetic past
for an unprecedented future
while poised present
It is so good to be
in the making of the moment

My heart is not a cemetery of dead things, dead men and dead relationships.
My heart is a verdant life spring. A seasoned garden, rejuvenating flowers and seeds of life.
Of rich soil, fertilizing buds to blossom.
My heart is not a cemetery of stone caskets holding withered vows and decayed promises.
Nor a sunken grave holding fallen words and perished feelings or fake bouquets.
Don't weep for me. I am not hopeless.
No. My heart overflows with beauty and compassion.
Brims with resilience and blithe.
It grows love. My heart is a safe place.
A forgiving place. A sentient landscape.
Gates welcoming and open. It is a well of life.
It is blessed and it is colorful!

and I learned that I'm blended beautifully...

with all the things that have happened to me
both with things I wanted and never wished for
with the things I said and didn't do
with all these feelings,
my hard parts and a little angel dust
with the prayers I cried and the laughs I smiled
with the people who came and the ones who left
with a little bit of malice and so much goodness
with the earth, the mud, and the sun
with everything and nothing
I am completely made of past or present
I know I am beautifully blended as me

A Declaration

I am unafraid to live
I look forward to my life
Though the moments are unpredictable and the days uncertain
I am sure
I remain confident in the grace that adorns me
I abide hopeful in the mercy that forbears
I resolve to awake and persist in the abundance of purpose
I awake to live in the prosperity of breath and love and joy
Because to not live fully is to discount the sac-
rifices and surrender of those before me
To not thrive wholly is to deaden the
prayers of the suppliants above me
Therefore,
I arise to give my all, to be roused by the gifts within me
I am unafraid to live;
I look forward to my life;
I will glory

What My Bones Know

Of brittle emotions once
    salient, once prominent
now hidden in marrow
    deep

Of movements graceful, young
    and sensual
once at ease, always peace

Days and accumulation of
    seasons and changes
my bones know of
    passing
of aging, of missing, of anticipating

My bones know of fear
    cloaked in skin
cloaked in denial and insecurity of
    the mortal inevitability

One day, these bones, to ash
    they will return as dust
in a warm cool breeze
    But
        until that day

The resilient spirit in me speaks
most audibly, quietly
triumphantly:

You could make this place beautiful

Again
   Daily
      Repeatedly

You could make beautiful
   in your womb
and you can curate a
brilliant sunshine from your heart

Truly navigate the terrain of
this (one chance) existence
tending carefully to steps
   barefoot
touching tenderly
the soft ones—we all are

My bones know
of red wine and yellow petals
   of dense white clouds
   and gravel
of salted tears and open arms

My bones know of living
   and dreaming
of wanting and clinging
   of believing and releasing
      of outliving and breathing

Emmanuella Raphaelle

My bones know
that while the body keeps score
the heart stops counting
and the heart furthers loving

Yes, the life, still
calls these bones to live

WORTHY WOMAN

Value

Value yourself
Value your loved ones and the tortured ones
Bring value to the room
all the ones you occupy,
each and every time at every table
Value the moments—they are fleeting
perishable and unrepeatable
Value the illumination and the dim
Value the peace and the chaos
Value the valley and the mountain
Value the you—you are
in every stage and season
Value your voice,
your visage,
your valor,
your versatility
and your vitality of living
Value your vessel, your being;
it is blessed

Value your values

Beloved,
Swallow your mustard seed
and speak faith
Swaddle your spirit in that faith
and be made whole

You are already well

When you were made in the watery grave of your mother's womb
it was dark, it was from love
and
when you were made into the person you have become today
it was dark, it was of love

But in the fullness of time
amid stars
you'll come to illuminate a new day
therefore, do not be afraid of the dark night threatening to stay

Because, Beloved, you should know
darkness is a promise that light is on the way

So then,
let there be light
let there be love

But
Love
is
trembling
and
trusting

Open your heart to real love.
It is profound.
It is sweet.
It is healing.

Darling,
do not hide your sensitivity
there is nothing to protect
you can still be loved and love
that you have not apprehended or obtained the prize…
is no indictment to you
and that is alright

There is beauty in your journey

May the morning taste delicious to you
and may it be truly new to you

May today break open to make way for you
yield promises for you
honor you

May the sky hold you in a pocket of air
protect your breath
inspire your life

May the bird's song sing to the worries in you,
serenade the affections in you
quiet the conflicts in you

May the soft rain shower you with delight
May the morning lend you more mercy
give you more grace

May the miracle of morning outlast you
And carry you all day

She craves...

more than four walls
she craves an open world
She craves a celebration of heritage
lessons etched in broken hearts free to live
She craves a fierce love to grip her insides
She craves passion
She craves the nerve to be her own woman
she craves her feelings
She craves curiosity
she craves the deep inside her deep
she craves imagination
dreams bigger than her visions
she craves courage
she craves the balance between
the sweet things and the sour things
she craves peace
she craves a different prayer
a universal language
she craves the heights
she craves beauty in the light
new beginnings
she craves the unknown
she craves wisdom of the bold
she craves dignity to live
her one worth-it life

She
sat down
in her quiet.
To hear her restless soul
speak.
She had
but one question for herself
and
she chastened herself
to hear the answer to
"Who Am I?"

And from rest and quiet,
her soul did speak,
to whisper the truth she did seek:

You are a divine and fallen beauty
A holy and mortal soul
Above all, you are His Beloved
And on you, His Favor rests
Be well in yourself

seek your heart,
Willow
surrender your innermost apology
intently
to every limb of your body
Love and loss renew you;
belonging in your strength
Your withstanding
yields a beautiful harmony
in hopeful healing

But Darling,
long before their eyes saw you
long before people came to love you,
to wound you
you were already the beloved
You were chosen for love
long before hurt, before pain
before rejection, before confusion...
You were loved
with a sensitive, safe love
an only reassuring
all covering love—
from above

Beg for no one's love--
You already are

Claim your Belovedness

*Nothing is new under the sun
or the soft fall of rain,...*

Therefore, do not allow
another thought in your pretty head
to convince you,
you are alone in this wonder-full world
picking up problems
and tripping over tribulations
You are never lonely in your longing
Grab your funkiest shades
or your brightest umbrella
Explore your surroundings
and welcome new solutions
You are not the only one in this time who did any particular thing!
Surrender self-judgment
Cognize yet still, there is good
Exalt your joy,
it is in you

Incurable

There are things within you, not on the outside,
needing your attention and affection, needing
your counseling and consoling.
Breathe into them.
There are things within you, not on the outside,
needing your peacetime into a sublime heart,
needing your praise and appraisal.
Love into them. Listen to them.
Let there be no conflict in you.
There are things within you, on the inside of you
Your sweetness and sorrow,
Your solace and suffering, take care of
Your sadness and happiness,
Your thrills and traumas, attend to
Do not discriminate, for you cannot segre-
gate the unwanted intervals of your life
You are to attend to the duality of your humanity
You cannot divorce yourself
Dear, go within
Cradle your wholeness
Along the days and ways to heal thyself
with devotion, will emerge your holy, healthy self
Know, all things are *in-cure-able*
Curable from your in…side
Let there be no di-vision in you

but you were never meant to be
a desolate place
for the nomads drifting
as fallen leaves
and lonely feathers;
you were always home and hearth
for the one love of your life

You

Beloved,
do not be disheartened or dispirited
Do not deprive from your body, confidence
or defer from your heart, hope
Do not stir up regret
or lose footing on your path
Through adversity and prosperity
It is all but for a season
for the greater making and preparing of
a victorious you
You alone are built for your life,
live it as only you can

Therefore, Darling
Please do not fight in your within
wrestling to unlearn the art of it;
un-loving won't work

Love lingers, therefore,
to bridge our disconnects,
to keep us gentle in the rough
and merciful in the mess of things

Accept that Love lingers
to remind us of our long-forgotten selves
when we were just babes in the belly of life
long before we learned to suckle words
and starve feelings

We were always born of a love undefiled
with a passionate purpose

Love lingers to keep us human

Emmanuella Raphaelle

Open the window
drink sunshine
stroll on a cloud
set your mind
fall in love with the day
wake up and live

Sunshine, I hope you woke up
with joy in your heart
and a song in your soul
because you were kept for this morning

Honey, I hope that when you woke up melancholy
you took a sip of the sunlight pouring outside
and refreshed yourself

And Love, I hope when you woke up this morning
you realized how fortunate you were
to open your eyes and breathe, yes, breathe

Above all, I hope you woke up this morning
with a mission to live
the intention to be well within, and
to give to yourself the greatest possible happiness you can,
You deserve it

She cares.
She cares about the words of others
and the language they use to shape her
the way they misname and misconstrue her
She cares,
though she knows not to.
She cares because she is human,
She is a woman becoming, evolving.
But she will learn to uncare
Because where she is going will require it!

When Spirit Speaks

Hello Beautiful…
Can you hear me?
I am here in the deep of your biology
living and moving in our being daily

I hear you talking about me
to your friends and family
as if I am not here

You speak words over me as if you forget I am near
to your heart
And too often, your voice does not speak well of me
So how am I to feel?

In the night, you murmur and pray through me
But how can I lift us up in prayer to the Master Creator
when you diminish His creativity?
By your ways, you insult His originality
I grieve in you as you despise me

I've seen you frown and snicker
Even avoid the mirror's reflection of *we*
Not at all encouraging
Not any bit of loving

And when it is morning, on a new day,
Hello Beautiful, I say
But your words are stained from yesterday
You cannot see our individuality, our eccentricity

as especially
We are no carbon copy;
we are His ingenuity

Darling, we've come a long way
from innocent youth to womanly wisdom
You've overlooked me at times
Hated me sometimes
Judged me too many times
And held me not enough times

You've criticized
the coarse…the blemish…the lines…
the stretch…the flesh…
all the parts you find flabby,
the long…the dark…the wrinkled…the straight…
the broad…the sagging…the hollow…
the natural
the bony…the pale …the scrawny…
the huge…the flat…the fat… the not so flat…
Who gave you these words to describe me?

You've put so many words on me
Never once asking me, what do I need…to be?
When the answer would always be
I need you to love me,
wholeheartedly, unconditionally, completely,
sincerely

Stop comparing me to airbrushed photography
and spoon-fed illusions of feminine grandiosity

Emmanuella Raphaelle

Know always
You are altogether beautiful, my Love,
there is no flaw in you
You are beautiful in your time,
with eternity nesting in your heart
Nothing on this Earth compares with you

You are the carrier of life and love,
the portal from the dark to the light
Risk being seen in all your glory
Because our Father in Heaven calls me:
Beloved
Precious, Gentle,
Delicate, Worthy, Blessed,
Splendid, Excellent, Faithful, Strong,
Virtuous, Dignified, Courageous, Kind, Powerful,
Valuable, Diligent, Full, Radiant,
Wise, Tender, Refined,
Royal, Chosen,
Loved

Therefore agree,
speaking nothing incongruent to our outwardly
Again, agree,
because all you say, we will be
So please, for our sake, speak kindly
When in doubt,
choose His words instead
Practice the art of affirming us daily

unfurl
your
fingers
one
by
one
until
you are
holding
nothing
but
air

this is how you live
let it all go
respire

Emmanuella Raphaelle

Woman,
you should get up and wash your face,
bathe the stench of him from your skin
rinse his scum from the creases of you
stop reading the writing on the bedroom walls
there is nothing new in the old paint
let the sun rewrite the tales of your heart
open the drapes
there is a different story to be given
novel words to be spoken in the midst
so, wipe the dust from the furniture,
change the sheets,
bless your bed
your change is within you
waiting on hope-full expression
consider yourself a publishing house
you are the author of your life
you are the founder of your love

True Story

She was tired, like an old woman
wearing faded knee highs around her ankles
smelling of smoked cigarettes forgotten
the burden of the world resting on her right shoulder
and on her left, the burden of lost love
digging like a thick bra strap uncomfortable
When will she love again?
Today she loves
She loves so good and strong
her youth returned to her
Her vigor, vibrant and vivacious
her appeal, seductive and real
She loves again
brimming to overflowing
from her innards to her inwards
surrounding
She loves repeatedly
daily, intentionally, intimately,
consistently

Undiminished

Your beauty is undiminished
Your love is undiminished
Your affection is undiminished
Your character is undiminished
Your faith is undiminished
Your joy is undiminished
Your creativity is undiminished
Your fervor is undiminished
Your strength is undiminished
Your devotion to self is undiminished
Your intelligence is undiminished
Your spirituality is undiminished
Your enthusiasm for life is undiminished
Your breath is undiminished
Your joi de vivre is undiminished
Your spirit to thrive is undiminished
Your resolve to evolve is undiminished
Your perseverance is undiminished
Your favor is undiminished
Your intensity is undiminished
Your passion is undiminished
Your character is undiminished
Your courage is undiminished
Your peace is undiminished
Your happiness is undiminished
Your influence is undiminished
Your vigor is undiminished
Your existence is undiminished
Your impact is undiminished

Your affect is undiminished
Your wisdom is undiminished
Your judgment is undiminished
Your sanity is undiminished
Your understanding is undiminished
Your trust is undiminished
Your hope is undiminished
Your will is undiminished
Your knowledge of self, in God, is undiminished
Your gentleness is undiminished
Your kindness is undiminished
Your calling is undiminished
Your purpose in life is undiminished
Your patience is undiminished
Your humility is undiminished
Your ambition is undiminished
Your aspiration is undiminished
Your confidence is undiminished
Your determination is undiminished
Your light is undiminished
Your liberty is undiminished
Your grace is undiminished
Your dignity is undiminished
Your goodness is undiminished
Your wellness is undiminished
Your thanksgiving is undiminished
Your gratefulness is undiminished
Your vision is undiminished
Your clarity is undiminished
Your purity of heart, of soul, of spirit—undiminished
Your laughter is undiminished

Emmanuella Raphaelle

Your gladness is undiminished
Your generosity of heart, love, & loyalty—undiminished
Your resilience is undiminished
Your love for life is undiminished

Through everything—You are Full of Life

[lahyf]

noun

1. the blessed breath that filled you to the brim when sunlight nudged you to look with new eyes upon this blank day. The verve to fill it in as only you please.

2. that amazing phenomenon that you carry within and give away with every word, smile, hug, good deed. The generous of your hands and heart poured out, into. Them. Others.

3. you, a reckless mess and eternal beauty; a beloved bouquet of impulse and passion planted in peace. A collection of moments and miracles bleeding beautiful in the shape of you.

Life wants you. Choose your life today.

POETIC POETRY

Embrace

Embrace your breath of life
Embrace the hope in your chest
Embrace your ambitions and your beliefs
Embrace the faith in your feet
Embrace your prayers and your affirmations
Embrace your power and your creativity
Embrace your suffering and your solace
Embrace your revelations and your knowing
Each one needs you; each one gifts you
Embrace your one true life

Emmanuella Raphaelle

Grace comes every day
New, waiting to fill full, hearts
Open your hope chest…

Flowering & Decaying

Love runs deep.
Undivided.
Spreading branches, reaching high
encompassing all
sinner to saint
time after time;
Fluttering
sunlight cascading,
pouring grace,
embracing all.
Divine love
roots compassion and
flowers unmerited mercy.
Always know, worthy are you

~ Beloved ~

you are worthy,
Know always,
mercy unmerited--flowers
and compassion roots love divine;
All-embracing...
Grace pouring,
cascading sunlight,
fluttering
time after time,
saint to sinner
All-encompassing,
High reaching, branches, spreading
undivided,
deep, runs love.

Emmanuella Raphaelle

I dreamed of wisdom and became wiser
Father God did make me to believe…
More than in my pocket, in my heart, is change
I see it in the daffodil's yellow
In the span of her wings, madame butterfly
She's writing with no words, a life song

A little bird hums from her heart a sublime love song
As wise fools eager, with age, we chance wiser
Life is measured, teaches the brilliant butterfly
Mother Nature learned me to believe
in the sky's blue, the blade's green, the sun's yellow
full heart, half-moon, how many stars, don't change

Time, leaves, skin, moments, all change
I still hear our sound in my head, like a favorite song
it stings like a bee but tastes sweet, like honey yellow
With every choice and every chance, I become wiser
In someday, in always, in now, I still believe
I spread my wings, take flight, and soar, beautiful butterfly

Protected in her cocoon, coming out, brave butterfly
Stagnant things painful, moving, so is change
Patience has a reward, this is what I believe
I've written words to live and dance in a new song
In the heart, vibrates peculiar lyrics, singing wiser
Life adores me, my happiness in the sunflower, yellow

The sum of all my memories reflect in golden yellow
In my pursuit for meaning, I found rest in the wing of the butterfly
Settled on my right shoulder, in that moment, I became wiser
Taught me an old lesson through every season and not once
did He change
Gives me a new strength, a new vision, a new thank you, a new song
A life of service, what you appreciate you give away, this I believe

I made a wish to the universe and promised to believe
to see beyond the gray, into the rainbow's yellow
to breath and move by my soul's sincere song
to break out into freedom like the intrepid butterfly
to walk humbly, boldly into my foretelling change
All of living, gifts, prompting us to incarnate wiser

As the butterfly lends her wings to floating through changes wiser,
we should believe in the song of our intuition
and the glorious yellow dreams to come

A Moment of Silence

It was a feeling that got lost in a cayenne sunset
wistfully pacing the rummages of slow footsteps in a forest
always leading her to a nostalgia steeped in the silver lake

Because anytime she felt a need to meditate,
her spirit led her to the lake
where she would sit to watch ripples bleed into the blurry sunset,
where her essence would rise up to feel at one
with the nature of the forest

There was a soft jazz hidden in the heart of the forest
a sweet sound that allowed her to dance with her
burdens on the surface of the lake
to leave them there with the bowing curtains
of the inevitable sunset

It was all she needed to recalibrate her reality, a solitary moment,
there, wrapped in the sunset, deep in the forest,
her thoughts wafting across the lake

The Body Keeps Score

It is said, the body keeps score
that if dry bones could speak, they might weep
and under soft skin, sinews, a sweet implore

Limbs drifting drowsy through threshold and door
beaming and mourning, coddling history from deep
It is said, the body keeps score

Of all things we love to adore, deem grotesque, and abhor
keep close, turn loose, donate, internal bleed to our beloveds, seep
and under soft skin, sinews, a sweet implore

To rise brilliant and resilient, from the ground floor
forgetting and remembering, a within voice counseling: boldly leap
It is said, the body keeps score

Until eyes remember light through every pore
reflecting pure love, because in peace divinity did steep
and under soft skin, sinews, a sweet implore

May you live triumphantly, vigorously, into grace galore
to the brink of the moment before the last exhale into eternal sleep
For it is said the body keeps score
and under soft skin, sinews, a sweet implore

Flowering & Decaying

Flesh cultivated for beauty, flourishing
Living to triumphantly fulfill
Our highest call to creatively express; oblivious while
Wrapped in a world of wonder, we press
Emerging petal by petal, we
Reach to reinvent selves to radiate
Inclined to individuate, inherited
Narratives coloring our motion, still
Grounded, growing, going with the seasons

And

Day by day, moment by memory, decreasing
Embracing the reality we've come unwound to the end of
Caring more and less about the minutia, colliding
Acknowledging all things don't share our meanings and
Youthful impulses humble us to wiser
Instincts to love and let…other lives live as
Now and now and now until we venture to rest
Gradually towards an inevitable glory

the air autumn-like
a light rain flirts with the sky
I stand here lonely
thirsty for raindrops that hold
promise: send me a rainbow

Emmanuella Raphaelle

Bound to my end, I love with everything
to let One Love, grow and forgive me.
Skin, bones, and marrow, heart, and flesh
to let pure Love pour in, through
Mask off, armor undone.
To behold within
beautiful eyes
given me
I have
Love

Natural Religion

They don't know I move mountains
Then find rest in the flourishing pasture's green
Sunflowers at my feet flirting with each breeze
Beauty deep waves crashing triumphantly, turquoise
Heart calm, mimicking rhythm with nature's melody
Nothing to lose, I plunge into surrender

Under the sea, eternity to sweet surrender
Flattened Earth, sans valleys, sans mountains
Brilliant sea creatures, swimming in melody
Tangled in floral coral reefs, immersed blue-green
Magic gems and swimming miracles, turquoise
Water navigating me, I float on a buoyant breeze

Dive into the air, I swallow a mouthful of tropical breeze
To fall limp and watch the world surrender
Embraced by the sun's warmth and cool water's turquoise
My chest rising and falling, resting on mounds of soft mountains
Plush seashore paspalum grass, bountiful leaves, green
I'm flying with Cuban Emeralds, humming in their melody

Gaze up, admiring the moon and the sun make melody
Wispy clouds slow-motion shifting in the gentle breeze
Setting down on Earth to touch the trees evergreen
Open arms, humble, I am nothing, soul surrender
Gratitude, He is everything, He moved my mountains
Adorned me in silk & a diadem of precious gems of turquoise

Emmanuella Raphaelle

Holding sunshine, soft sands, treasuring turquoise
Newfound serenity composes my body melody
I move gracefully, stand, to pose with the mountain
Inhale goodness, exhale mercy, dwelling in the breeze
Love caught up, captured me in a blessed surrender
Among affectionate garden roses, orchids, daylilies, plush greens

A calm refugee, under folds of a Guadeloupe palm tree, green
I bask in the cures of nature's translucence, blues & turquoise
All of my will submits to stolen surrender
Freedom generates, resonates a percussion of romantic melody
For strolling upon soft Earth is a Bahama breeze
From oceanside to the peak, I am friends with the mountain

Peace is in the center of the mountain and pasture's green
In the chase of the breeze, nestled in the jewel of turquoise
Resting in heart's melody; Everything a sweet, mysterious surrender

Flowering & Decaying

life is so beautiful in the rain
love is so wonderful when pure
sunshine belongs on your skin
the blues tempers the heart
good music is food
dreams do come true
grace abounds
joy lasts
breathe

Lesson of the Leaves

Stand under an autumn-colored tree
to watch the Fall of prodigal leaves
and witness how Earth lets go of attachments un-necessary
See how the tree takes her time...
tarries in vulnerability
to create room for growth
For all new things to come
Trusting right timing and right endowing
Trusting in He who sent His word once
And Earth believed unceasingly
to abide and agree forevermore

Darling, there will always be a chore, no matter *what*,
the busy things will summon, still exert your *will*.
Dare, examine and experience what dances in *you*
be it ordinary or extraordinary in all you *do*;
Find the song you love to sing along *with*
and let it carry you from day to day in all *your*
doing, being, working, running, loving as *one*
woman afraid, courageous, cautious, learning, *wild*.
Make time to seek the intermissions, the interludes *and*
pause to pray and relish in real time over the *precious*
For these are the beautiful days of your best *life*.

Leap into a lifted rest to both *offer* and obtain
a gift of transcendent *value* whence life is
worthy of your full emphatic *embrace*

LOVE

EPILOGUE

This is Your Life

Hello mother, sister, daughter, darling, friend and beloved,
I need you to know something,
really need you to get this deep down in your bowels
This is not your practice life, not make-be-
lieve, nor the one you pretend to have—
Woman, this is your life!

This is your one and only never again to breathe life--Now
And in this one precious life—you will have many
variations to live and give, to grow and flow
with the cadence and undulations of life
Give in.

I know at times it has been an incredible mess of things,
a compilation of blessings and unimaginable things,
completely disorganized yet orderly
cause it takes time and living to truly know, all things
work unceasingly for your absolute and perfect good

Some days you'll have it all together
your bag and shoes will match, and your shit won't stink
and you'll have confidence taller than a magnolia tree
You'll believe the sun rose to shine the day for you brilliantly
and all the plans you put your hands to
will work with almost magical impeccability

But on other days—yes, there will be them other days
when you'll be doubting and praying; cursing and hoping

A bloody, sweaty pile of emotions and impulses craving a miracle
questioning the system of things

And the moon's glow will soften the blow,
fade into the night decisions of the day
And it will still be your life

You'll be a walking contradiction
reconciling and discovering with every step
You can choose, you can change, you can take charge
you are your champion--Now

And thank God for grace
for pardoning and forgiveness
for second chances and a few more chances
for charity,
for clarity in belonging
in your life now
Surrender into your deity

Now is the time to do the damn thing, to
take the chance and regret nothing
Now is the time to know and go, to change
your mind, to rethink your ways
Now is the time to be happy, to count your
blessings, and reframe your burdens
Now is the time to love and be loved,
to give a kind word, to be and grow in community
to be free, to be limitless,
to be your whole self

May you have peace and serenity
to claim your life
Own your stuff,
you have the ability and the artistry
Breathe in divine authority to live, love, and accept
your one real life
now

Now is full with favor, now is the right time

An ENTRY

These days, our sisterhood is a little more private, a little more intimate, and a lot different from how it used to be.

At the beginning of each day, early after sunrise, a 'Good Morning' text to bless the happenings of the day is sent to one another.

We agreed, and we chose the first weekend of each month to continue in *our* together. To do the cool things sisters do, like eat brunch and window shop. Like making candles and fine dining. Or walk up and down the quaint streets of Savannah, marvel at the weeping trees, and peek into locally owned shops.

In our together, we laugh and talk and reflect. Most of all, we relate as two individual women from the same womb. As sisters and women becoming, we swap self-full stories and revelations. She is seeking change and making moves. She is self-caring. She is emerging.

We share our mother--she more weekends than I. We continue to live in the gap of where love was once in the shape of *her*.

Today, she is dust in a royal blue urn, embellished with silver butterflies, sitting at my fireplace. Soon we will travel to scatter her ashes and remember her beauty. Though she is gone, we are not without her. We are propelled to live.

I am encouraged to make good on what she believed of me. She aspired to share her words with the world. I give them for her. We live them for her.

At the end of the day and the beginning of the next, we are grateful. We are fine. We make plans to travel and drink wine.

To every sister, who came, and who remains. Do not miss your life. Remember, hold the hand of another sister while you can.

ABOUT THE AUTHOR

My honesty, my beauty, my peculiarity
my love, my joy, my need, my pain…
These are what I know; of them is what I write
I'd love to make up other things, but it is not of me
Life inspires me; God grants me; words free me.

Child of God; woman becoming.
Daughter, sister, friend, mother.
Mentor, encourager, disruptor.
Dreamer, achiever.

Author. Lover. Inspirer.